Euripides

Bacchae

Translated
by
Ian Johnston
Malaspina University-College
Nanaimo, British Columbia
Canada

Richer Resources Publications
Arlington, Virginia
USA

Euripides
Bacchae

Reprint requests and requests for additional copies of this book
should be addressed to

Richer Resources Publications
1926 N. Woodrow Street
Arlington, Virginia 22207
or via our web site at
www.RicherResourcesPublications.com

ISBN 978-0-9797571-2-9
Library of Congress Control Number 2007937531

Published by Richer Resources Publications
Arlington, Virginia
Printed in the United States of America

Euripides
Bacchae

Translator's Note

The translator would like to acknowledge the valuable help of E. R. Dodds' edition of and commentary on the Bacchae (Oxford, 1960).

Note that the normal line numbers refer to this text and the ones in square brackets refer to the lines in the Greek text. There is an important gap of 50 lines or more in Euripides' manuscript between lines 1329 and 1330 of the Greek text. The content of the missing lines is fairly well known, so this translation has attempted to provide a reconstructed text for the missing portion (lines 1645 to 1699 of the English text). That reconstructed text appears between square brackets. For a brief account of the missing material see Dodds p. 234.

For a brief interpretative introduction to *The Bacchae* consult the follow link on the Internet: http://www.mala.bc.ca/~johnstoi/ euripides/Bacchae_Introduction.htm

A Note on the Author

Euripides (born c. 484 in Athens) wrote a number of plays and won first prize in the competition for tragedy five times. The majority of these works have not survived. It is clear from comments in other works (especially in the plays of Aristophanes) that Euripides was a controversial figure in Athens. In 408 he moved from Athens to Macdonia and died the following year, allegedly torn apart by a pack of hunting dogs. *The Bacchae*, one of his last plays, was not performed during his lifetime.

Bacchae
Dramatis Personae

DIONYSUS: divine son of Zeus and Semele.

TIRESIAS: an old blind prophet.

CADMUS: grandfather of both Dionysus and Pentheus, an old man.

PENTHEUS: young king of Thebes, grandson of Cadmus, cousin of Dionysus.

AGAVE: mother of Pentheus, daughter of Cadmus, sister of Semele.

FIRST MESSENGER: a cattle herder.

SECOND MESSENGER: an attendant on Pentheus.

CHORUS OF BACCHAE: worshippers of Dionysus who have followed him from Asia, also called Maenads or Bacchants.

SOLDIERS and ATTENDANTS around Pentheus.

[The action takes place in front of the royal palace of Thebes. Enter DIONYSUS]

DIONYSUS
    I've arrived here in the land of Thebes,
    I, Dionysus, son of Zeus, born to him
    from Semele, Cadmus' daughter, delivered
    by a fiery midwife—Zeus' lightning flash.[1]
    Yes, I've changed my form from god to human,
    appearing here at these streams of Dirce,
    the waters of Ismenus. I see my mother's tomb—
    for she was wiped out by that lightning bolt.
    It's there, by the palace, with that rubble,

---

[1] Semele, Cadmus' daughter and Dionysus' mother, had an affair with Zeus. Hera, Zeus' wife, tricked Zeus into destroying Semele with a lightning bolt. Zeus took Dionysus and concealed him in his thigh to hide him from Hera.

the remnants of her house, still smoldering   10
from Zeus' living fire—Hera's undying outrage
against my mother. But I praise Cadmus.   [10]
He's made his daughter's shrine a sacred place.
I have myself completely covered it
with leafy shoots of grape-bearing vines.
I've left the fabulously wealthy East,
lands of Lydians and Phrygians,
Persia's sun-drenched plains, walled towns in Bactria.
I've moved across the bleak lands of the Medes,
through rich Arabia, all Asian lands,   20
along the salt-sea coast, through those cities
with their beautifully constructed towers,
full of barbarians and Greeks all intermingled.
Now I've come to Thebes, city of Greeks,   [20]
only after I've set those eastern lands
dancing in the mysteries I established,
making known to men my own divinity.
Thebes is the first city of the Greeks
where I've roused people to shout out my cries,
with this deerskin draped around my body,   30
this ivy spear, a thyrsus, in my hand.[1]
For my mother's sisters have acted badly,
something they, of all people, should avoid.
They stated aloud that I, Dionysus,
was no child of Zeus, claiming Semele,
once she was pregnant by some mortal man,
attributed her bad luck in bed to Zeus,
a story made up (they said) to trick Cadmus.   [30]
Those sisters state that's why Zeus killed her,
because she lied about the man she'd slept with.   40
So I've driven those women from their homes
in a frenzy—they now live in the mountains,

---

[1]A thyrsus (pl. thyrsoi) is a hollow plant stalk, usually decorated with ivy, and
carried as a symbol of Dionysus in the dancing celebrations (where it can
acquire magical powers).

6

out of their minds. I've made them put on costumes,
outfits appropriate for my mysteries.
All Theban offspring—or, at least, all women—
I've driven in a crazed fit from their homes.
Now they sit out there among the rocks,
underneath green pine trees, no roof overhead,
Cadmus' daughters in their company as well.
For this city has to learn, though against its will,   50
that it has yet to be initiated
into my Dionysian rites. Here I plead   [40]
the cause of my own mother, Semele,
appearing as a god to mortal men,
the one she bore to Zeus. Now Cadmus,
the old king, has just transferred his power,
his royal authority, to Pentheus,
his daughter's son, who, in my case at least,
fights against the gods, prohibiting me
all sacrificial offerings. When he prays,   60
he chooses to ignore me. For this neglect
I'll demonstrate to him, to all in Thebes,
that I was born a god. Once these things here
have been made right, I'll move on somewhere else,
to some other land, revealing who I am.
But if Thebans in this city, in their anger,   [50]
try to make those Bacchic women leave,
to drive them from the mountains forcibly,
then I, commander of these Maenads,
will fight them.[1] That's why I've transformed myself,   70
assumed a mortal shape, altered my looks,
so I resemble any human being.

*[Enter the Chorus of Bacchae, dressed in ritual deerskin, carrying
small drums like tambourines]*

But you there, you women who've left Tmolus,

---

[1]The Maenads, who make up the Chorus in the play, are the female followers of
Dionysus, who have come with him from the east, from Phrygia in Asia Minor.

backbone of Lydia, my band of worshippers,
whom I've led here from barbarian lands,
my comrades on the road and when we rest,
take up your drums, those instruments of yours
from Phrygian cities, first invented
by mother Rhea and myself.[1] Move round here,
beat those drums by Pentheus' palace,   80   [60]
let Cadmus' city see you, while I go,
in person, to the clefts of Mount Cithaeron,
to my Bacchae, to join their dancing.

[Exit Dionysus]

CHORUS *[singing and dancing]*

FIRST VOICE
From Asia, from sacred Tmolus
I've come to dance,
to move swiftly in my dance—
for Bromius—
sweet and easy task,
to cry out in celebration,
hailing great god Bacchus.[2]   90

SECOND VOICE
Who's in the street? Who's there? Who?
Let him stay inside
out of our way.
Let every mouth be pure,   [70]
completely holy,
speak no profanities.
In my hymn I celebrate
our old eternal custom,
hailing Dionysus.

---

[1]Rhea is Zeus' mother. The drums referred to are like tambourines. Tmolus is a
river in Asia Minor.

[2]Bromius and Bacchus are alternative names for Dionysus.

8

THIRD VOICE

O, blessed is the man,   100
the fortunate man who knows
the rituals of the gods,
who leads a pious life,
whose spirit merges
with these Bacchic celebrations,
frenzied dancing in the mountains,
our purifying rites—
one who reveres these mysteries
from Cybele, our great mother,
who, waving the thyrsus,   110   [80]
forehead crowned with ivy,
serves Dionysus.[1]

FOURTH VOICE

On Bacchae! Bacchae, move!
Bring home Bromius, our god,
son of god, great Dionysus,
from Phrygian mountains
to spacious roads of Greece—
Hail Bromius!

FIFTH VOICE

His mother dropped him early,
as her womb, in forceful birth pangs,   120
was struck by Zeus' flying lightning bolt,   [90]
a blast which took her life.
Then Zeus, son of Cronos,
at once hid him away
in a secret birthing chamber,
buried in his thigh,
shut in with golden clasps,
concealed from Hera.

[1]Cybele is an eastern mother goddess.

9

SIXTH VOICE

Fates made him perfect.
Then Zeus gave birth to him,   130   [100]
the god with ox's horns,
crowned with wreaths of snakes—
that's why the Maenads
twist in their hair
wild snakes they capture.

SEVENTH VOICE

O Thebes, nursemaid of Semele,
put on your ivy crown,
flaunt your green yew,
flaunt its sweet fruit!
Consecrate yourselves to Bacchus,   140
with stems of oak or fir,   [110]
Dress yourselves in spotted fawn skins,
trimmed with white sheep's wool.
As you wave your thyrsus,
revere the violence it contains.
All the earth will dance at once.
Whoever leads our dancing—
that one is Bromius!
To the mountain, to the mountain,
where the pack of women waits,   150
all stung to frenzied madness
to leave their weaving shuttles,
goaded on by Dionysus.

EIGHTH VOICE

O you dark chambers of the Curetes,   [120]
you sacred caves in Crete,
birthplace of Zeus,
where the Corybantes in their caves,
men with triple helmets, made for me

10

this circle of stretched hide.[1]
In their wild ecstatic dancing,   160
they mixed this drum beat
with the sweet seductive tones
of flutes from Phrygia,
then gave it to mother Rhea
to beat time for the Bacchae,
when they sang in ecstasy.
Nearby, orgiastic satyrs,   [130]
in ritual worship of the mother goddess,
took that drum, then brought it
into their biennial dance,   170
bringing joy to Dionysus.

NINTH VOICE
He's welcome in the mountains,
when he sinks down to the ground,
after the running dance,
wrapped in holy deerskin,
hunting the goat's blood,
blood of the slain beast,
devouring its raw flesh with joy,
rushing off into the mountains,
in Phrygia, in Lydia,   180   [140]
leading the dance—
Bromius—Evoe![2]

ALL
The land flows with milk,
the land flows with wine,
the land flows with honey from the bees.
He holds the torch up high,
our leader, the Bacchic One,

[1]The Curetes and Corybantes are attendants on the goddess Cybele. They
banged their drums to drown out the cries of the infant Zeus, whom Rhea was
hiding in a cave on Crete to protect him from his father Cronos.

[2]Evoë is a cry of celebration in the Bacchic rituals.

11

blazing flame of pine,
sweet smoke like Syrian incense,
trailing from his thyrsus. 190
As he dances, he runs,
here and there,
rousing the stragglers,
stirring them with his cries,
thick hair rippling in the breeze. [150]
Among the Maenads' shouts
his voice reverberates:
"On Bacchants, on!
With the glitter of Tmolus,
which flows with gold, 200
chant songs to Dionysus,
to the loud beat of our drums.
Celebrate the god of joy
with your own joy,
with Phrygian cries and shouts!
When sweet sacred pipes [160]
play out their rhythmic holy song,
in time to the dancing wanderers,
then to the mountains,
on, on to the mountains." 210
Then the bacchanalian woman
is filled with total joy—
like a foal in pasture
right beside her mother—
her swift feet skip in playful dance.

[Enter Tiresias, a very old blind man, dressed in clothing appropriate for the Dionysian ritual. He goes up to the palace door and knocks very aggressively]

TIRESIAS *[shouting]*
　　Where's the servant on the door? You in there, [170]
　　tell Cadmus to get himself out of the house,
　　Agenor's lad, who came here from Sidon,

12

then put up the towers of this Theban town.[1]
Go tell him Tiresias is waiting for him.   220
He knows well enough why I've come for him.
I'm an old man, and he's even older,
but we've agreed make ourselves a thyrsus,
to put on fawn skins and crown our heads
with garlands of these ivy branches.

*[Enter Cadmus from the palace, a very old man, also dressed in
clothing appropriate for the Dionysian ritual]*

CADMUS
                    My dearest friend,
I was inside the house. I heard your voice.
I recognized it—the voice of a man truly wise.
So I've come equipped with all this god stuff.   [180]
We must sing his praise, as much as we can,
for this Dionysus, well, he's my daughter's child.   230
Now he's revealed himself a god to men.
Where must I go and dance? Where do I get
to move my feet and shake my old gray head?
You must guide me, Tiresias, one old man
leading another, for you're the expert here.
O, I'll never tire of waving this thyrsus,
day and night, striking the ground. What rapture!
Now we can forget that we're old men.

TIRESIAS
You feel the same way I do, then.
For I'm young and going to try the dancing.   240   [190]

CADMUS
Shall we go up the mountain in a chariot?

TIRESIAS
The god would not then get complete respect.

[1]Sidon, in Asia Minor, as these lines inform us, was the place where the Theban
royal family originated.

13

CADMUS
So I'll be your nursemaid—one old man
will take charge of another one?

TIRESIAS
                              The god himself
will get us to the place without our efforts.

CADMUS
Of all the city are we the only ones
who'll dance to honour Bacchus?

TIRESIAS
                              Yes, indeed,
for we're the only ones whose minds are clear.
As for the others, well, their thinking's wrong.

CADMUS
We should not wait too long. Take my hand.   250

TIRESIAS *[holding out his hand]*
Here. Take it—make a pair of it and yours.

CADMUS
I'm a mortal, so I don't mock the gods.

TIRESIAS
To the gods we mortals are all ignorant.   [200]
Those old traditions from our ancestors,
the ones we've had as long as time itself,
no argument will ever overthrow,
in spite of subtleties sharp minds invent.
Will someone say I disrespect old age,
if I intend to dance with ivy on my head?
Not so, for the god makes no distinctions—   260
whether the dancing is for young or old.
He wants to gather honours from us all,
to be praised communally, without division.

14

CADMUS
Since you're blind to daylight, Tiresias,   [210]
I'll be your seer, tell you what's going on—
Pentheus, that child of Echion, the one
to whom I handed over power in this land,
he's coming here, to the house. He's in a rush.
He looks so flustered. What news will he bring?

[Enter Pentheus, with some armed attendants. At first he does not notice Cadmus and Tiresias, not until he calls attention to them]

PENTHEUS
It so happens I've been away from Thebes,   270
but I hear about disgusting things going on,
here in the city—women leaving home
to go to silly Bacchic rituals,
cavorting there in mountain shadows,
with dances honouring some upstart god,
this Dionysus, whoever he may be. Mixing bowls   [220]
in the middle of their meetings filled with wine,
they creep off one by one to lonely spots
to have sex with men, claiming they're Maenads
busy worshipping. But they rank Aphrodite,   280
goddess of sexual desire, ahead of Bacchus.
All the ones I've caught, my servants guard
in our public prison, their hands chained up.
All those who're still away I will chase down,
hunt them from the mountains—that includes
Agave, who bore me to Echion, Ino,
and Autonoe, Actaeon's mother.[1]   [230]
Once I've clamped them all in iron fetters,
I'll quickly end this perverse nastiness,
this Bacchic celebration. People say   290
some stranger has arrived, some wizard,

[1]Actaeon, son of Autonoe and Aristaeus, offended the goddess Artemis (the reasons vary from one version of his story to another). The goddess had him destroyed by his own hunting dogs. See line 420 below.

15

a conjurer from the land of Lydia,
with sweet-smelling hair in golden ringlets
and Aphrodite's charms in wine-dark eyes.
He hangs around the young girls day and night,
dangling in front of them his joyful mysteries.
If I catch him in this city, I'll stop him.
He'll make no more clatter with his thyrsus,   [240]
or wave his hair around. I'll chop off his head,
slice it right from his body. This man claims   300
that Dionysus is a god, alleging
that once upon a time he was sewn up,
stitched inside Zeus' thigh—but Dionysus
was burned to death, along with Semele,
in that lightning strike, because she'd lied.
She maintained that she'd had sex with Zeus.
All this surely merits harsh punishment,
death by hanging. Whoever this stranger is,
his insolence is an insult to me.

[Pentheus notices Cadmus and Tiresias for the first time]

Well, here's something totally astounding!   310
I see Tiresias, our soothsayer, all dressed up
in dappled fawn skins—my mother's father, too!   [250]
This is ridiculous. To take a thyrsus
and prance around like this. *[To Cadmus]* You sir,
I don't like to see such arrant foolishness
from your old age. Why not throw out that ivy?
And, grandfather, why not let that thyrsus go?

[Turning to address Tiresias]

Tiresias, you're the one who's put him up to this.
You want to bring in some new god for men,
so you'll be able to inspect more birds,   320
and from his sacrifices make more money.
If your gray old age did not protect you,
you'd sit in chains with all the Bacchae

16

for such a ceremonial perversion.   [260]
Whenever women at some banquet
start to take pleasure in the gleaming wine,
I say there's nothing healthy in their worship.

CHORUS LEADER
    That's impiety! O stranger,
    have you no reverence for the gods, for Cadmus,
    who sowed that crop of men born from the earth?[1]   330
    You're a child of Echion—do you wish
    to bring your own family into disrepute?

TIRESIAS
    When a man of wisdom has good occasion
    to speak out and takes the opportunity,
    it's not that hard to give an excellent speech.
    You've got a quick tongue and seem intelligent,
    but your words don't make any sense at all.
    A fluent orator whose power comes   [270]
    from self-assurance and from nothing else
    makes a bad citizen, for he lacks sense.   340
    This man, this new god, whom you ridicule—
    it's impossible for me to tell you
    just how great he'll be in all of Greece.
    Young man, among human beings two things
    stand out preeminent, of highest rank.
    Goddess Demeter is one—she's the earth
    (though you can call her any name you wish),
    and she feeds mortal people cereal grains.
    The other one came later, born of Semele—
    he brought with him liquor from the grape,   350
    something to match the bread from Demeter.
    He introduced it among mortal men.
    When they can drink up what streams off the vine,
    unhappy mortals are released from pain.   [280]

---

[1]According to legend, Cadmus killed a dragon and sowed its teeth into the
earth. They grew out of the soil as armed warriors. See line 1270 below.

17

It grants them sleep, allows them to forget
their daily troubles. Apart from wine,
there is no cure for human hardship.
He, being a god, is poured out to the gods,
so human beings receive fine benefits
as gifts from him. And yet you mock him. Why?   360
Because he was sewn into Zeus thigh?
Well, I'll show you how this all makes sense.
When Zeus grabbed him from the lightning flame,
he brought him to Olympus as a god.
But Hera wished to throw him out of heaven.   [290]
So Zeus, in a manner worthy of a god,
came up with a cunning counter plan.
From the sky which flows around the earth,
Zeus broke off a piece, shaped it like Dionysus,
then gave that to Hera, as a hostage.   370
The real child he sent to nymphs to raise,
thus saving him from Hera's jealousy.
Over time people mixed up "sky" and "thigh,"
saying he'd come from Zeus's thigh, changing words,
because he, a god, had once been hostage
to goddess Hera. So they made up the tale.
This god's a prophet, too, for in his rites—
the Bacchic celebrations and the madness—
a huge prophetic power is unleashed.
When the god fully enters human bodies,   380   [300]
he makes those possessed by frenzy prophets.
They speak of what will come in future days.
He also shares the work of war god Ares.
For there are times an army all drawn up,
its weapons ready, can shake with terror,
before any man has set hand to his spear.
Such madness comes from Dionysus.
Some day you'll see him on those rocks at Delphi,
leaping with torches on the higher slopes,
way up there between two mountain peaks,   390

waving and shaking his Bacchic wand,
a great power in Greece. Trust me, Pentheus.
Don't be too confident a sovereign's force
controls men. If something seems right to you,   [310]
but your mind's diseased, don't think that's wisdom.
So welcome this god into your country.
Pour libations to him, then celebrate
these Bacchic rites with garlands on your head.
On women, where Aphrodite is concerned,
Dionysus will not enforce restraint—   400
such modesty you must seek in nature,
where it already dwells. For any woman
whose character is chaste won't be defiled
by Bacchic revelry. Don't you see that?
When there are many people at your gates,
you're happy. The city shouts your praise.
It celebrates the name of Pentheus.   [320]
The god, too, I think, derives great pleasure
from being honoured. And so Cadmus,
whom you mock, and I will crown our heads   410
with ivy and will join the ritual,
an old gray team, but still we have to dance.
Your words will not turn me against the god,
for you are mad, under a cruel delusion.
No drug can heal that ailment—in fact,
some drug has caused it

CHORUS LEADER

Old man,
you've not disgraced Apollo with your words,
and by honouring this Dionysus,
a great god, you show your moderation.

CADMUS

My child, Tiresias has given you   420 [330]
some good advice. You should live among us,
not outside traditions. At this point,

19

you're flying around—thinking, but not clearly.
For if, as you claim, this man is not a god,
why not call him one? Why not tell a lie,
a really good one? Then it will seem
that some god has been born to Semele.
We—and all our family—will win honour.
Remember the dismal fate of Actaeon—
torn to pieces in some mountain forest   430
by blood-thirsty dogs he'd raised himself.
He'd boasted he was better in the hunt   [340]
than Artemis. Don't suffer the same fate.
Come here. Let me crown your head with ivy.
Join us in giving honour to this god.

PENTHEUS
Keep your hands off me! Be off with you—
go to these Bacchic rituals of yours.
But don't infect me with your madness.
As for the one who in this foolishness
has been your teacher, I'll bring him to justice.   440

[To his attendants]

One of you, go quickly to where this man,
Tiresias, has that seat of his, the place
where he inspects his birds. Take some levers,
knock it down. Demolish it completely.
Turn the whole place upside down—all of it.
Let his holy ribbons fly off in the winds.   [350]
That way I'll really do him damage.
You others—go to the city, scour it
to capture this effeminate stranger,
who corrupts our women with a new disease,   450
and thus infects our beds. If you get him,
tie him up and bring him here for judgment,
a death by stoning. That way he'll see
his rites in Thebes come to a bitter end.

20

[Exit Pentheus into the palace]

TIRESIAS
You unhappy man, you've no idea
just what it is you're saying. You've gone mad!
Even before now you weren't in your right mind.
Let's be off, Cadmus. We'll pray to the god   [360]
on Pentheus' behalf, though he's a savage,
and for the city, too, so he won't harm it.   460
Come with me—bring the ivy-covered staff.
See if you can help support my body.
I'll do the same for you. It would be shameful
if two old men collapsed. No matter—
for we must serve Bacchus, son of Zeus.
But you, Cadmus, you should be more careful,
or Pentheus will bring trouble in your home.
I'm not saying this as a prophecy,
but on the basis of what's going on.
A man who's mad tends to utter madness.   470

[Exit Tiresias and Cadmus together on their way to the mountains]

CHORUS
Holiness, queen of the gods,   [370]
Holiness, sweeping over earth
on wings of gold,
do you hear what Pentheus says?
Do you hear the profanities he utters,
the insults against Bromius,
child of Semele, chief god
among all blessed gods,
for those who wear their lovely garlands
in a spirit of harmonious joy?   480
This is his special office,
to lead men together in the dance,
to make them laugh as the flute plays,   [380]
to bring all sorrows to an end,

21

at the god's sacrificial feast,
when the gleaming liquid grapes arrive,
when the wine bowl casts its sleep
on ivy-covered feasting men.

Unbridled tongues and lawless folly
come to an end only in disaster.   490
A peaceful life of wisdom   [390]
maintains tranquillity.
It keeps the home united.
Though gods live in the sky,
from far away in heaven
they gaze upon the deeds of men.
But being clever isn't wisdom.
And thinking deeply about things
isn't suitable for mortal men.
Our life is brief—that's why   500
the man who chases greatness
fails to grasp what's near at hand.
That's what madmen do,   [400]
men who've lost their wits.
That's what I believe.

Would I might go to Cyprus,
island of Aphrodite,
where the Erotes,
bewitching goddesses of love,
soothe the hearts of humankind,   510
or to Paphos, rich and fertile,
not with rain, but with the waters
of a hundred flowing mouths
of a strange and foreign river.
O Bromius, Bromius,
inspired god who leads the Bacchae,
lead me away to lovely Peira,   [410]
where Muses dwell,
or to Olympus' sacred slopes,

22

where Graces live, Desire, too,   520
where it's lawful and appropriate
to celebrate our rites with Bacchus.

This god, the son of Zeus,
rejoices in our banquets.
He adores the goddess Peace,
and she brings riches with her   [420]
and nourishes the young.
The god gives his wine equally,
sharing with rich and poor alike.
It takes away all sorrow.   530
But he hates the man who doesn't care
to live his life in happiness,
by day and through the friendly nights.
From those who deny such common things
he removes intelligence,
their knowledge of true wisdom.
So I take this as my rule—
follow what common people think—   [430]
do what most men do.

[Enter a group of soldiers, bringing Dionysus with his arms tied up.
Pentheus enters from the palace]

SOLDIER

Pentheus, we're here because we've caught the prey   540
you sent us out to catch. Yes, our attempts
have proved successful. The beast you see here
was tame with us. He didn't try to run.
No, he surrendered willingly enough,
without turning pale or changing colour
on those wine dark cheeks. He even laughed at us,
inviting us to tie him up and lead him off.   [440]
He stood still, making it easier for me
to take him in. It was awkward, so I said,
"Stranger, I don't want to lead you off,   550

23

but I'm under orders here from Pentheus,
who sent me." And there's something else—
those Bacchic women you locked up, the ones
you took in chains into the public prison—
they've all escaped. They're gone—playing around
in some meadow, calling out to Bromius,
summoning their god. Chains fell off their feet,
just dropping on their own. Keys opened doors
not turned by human hands. This man here
has come to Thebes full of amazing tricks.   560
But now the rest of this affair is up to you.   [450]

*[Soldier hands chained Dionysus over to Pentheus, who moves up
close to Dionysus, inspecting him carefully]*

PENTHEUS
Untie his hands. I've got him in my nets.
He's not fast enough to get away from me.

*[Soldiers remove the chains from Dionysus' hands. Pentheus moves
in closer]*

Well, stranger, I see this body of yours
is not unsuitable for women's pleasure—
that's why you've come to Thebes. As for your hair,
it's long, which suggests that you're no wrestler.
It flows across your cheeks   That's most seductive.
You've a white skin, too. You've looked after it,
avoiding the sun's rays by staying in the shade,   570
while with your beauty you chase Aphrodite.
But first tell me something of your family.   [460]

DIONYSUS
That's easy enough, though I'm not boasting.
You've heard of the Tmolus, where flowers grow.

PENTHEUS
I know it. It's around the town of Sardis.

24

DIONYSUS
I'm from there. My home land is Lydia.

PENTHEUS
Why do you bring these rituals to Greece?

DIONYSUS
Dionysus sent me—the son of Zeus.

PENTHEUS
Is there some Zeus there who creates new gods?

DIONYSUS
No. It's the same Zeus who wed Semele right here.   580

PENTHEUS
Did this Zeus overpower you at night,
in your dreams? Or were your eyes wide open?

DIONYSUS
I saw him—he saw me. He handed me   [470]
the sacred rituals.

PENTHEUS
                    Tell me what they're like,
these rituals of yours.

DIONYSUS
                    That information
cannot be passed on to men like you,
those uninitiated in the rites of Bacchus.

PENTHEUS
Do they benefit those who sacrifice?

DIONYSUS
They're worth knowing, but you're not allowed to hear.

PENTHEUS
You've avoided that question skilfully,   590

25

making me want to hear an answer.

DIONYSUS
The rituals are no friend of any man
who's hostile to the gods.

PENTHEUS
                              This god of yours,
since you saw him clearly, what's he like?

DIONYSUS
He was what he wished to be, not made to order.

PENTHEUS
Again you glibly evade my question,
saying nothing whatsoever.

DIONYSUS
                              Yes, but then
a man can seem totally ignorant
when speaking to a fool.   [480]

PENTHEUS
                              Is Thebes
the first place you've come to with your god?   600

DIONYSUS
All the barbarians are dancing in these rites.

PENTHEUS
I'm not surprised. They're stupider than Greeks.

DIONYSUS
In this they are much wiser. But their laws
are very different, too.

PENTHEUS
                    When you dance these rites,
is it at night or during daylight hours?

26

DIONYSUS
Mainly at night. Shadows confer solemnity.

PENTHEUS
And deceive the women. It's all corrupt!

DIONYSUS
One can do shameful things in daylight, too.

PENTHEUS
You must be punished for these evil games.

DIONYSUS
You, too—for foolishness, impiety   610
towards the god.   [490]

PENTHEUS
                     How brash this Bacchant is!
How well prepared in using language!

DIONYSUS
What punishment am I to suffer?
What harsh penalties will you inflict?

PENTHEUS
First, I'll cut off this delicate hair of yours.

DIONYSUS
My hair is sacred. I grow it for the god.

PENTHEUS
And give me that thyrsus in your hand.

DIONYSUS
This wand I carry is the god's, not mine.
You'll have to seize it from me for yourself.

PENTHEUS
We'll lock your body up inside, in prison.   620

27

DIONYSUS
The god will personally set me free,
whenever I so choose.

PENTHEUS
                    That only works
if you call him while among the Bacchae.

DIONYSUS
He sees my suffering now—and from near by.   [500]

PENTHEUS
Where is he then? My eyes don't see him.

DIONYSUS
He's where I am. You can't see him,
because you don't believe.

PENTHEUS *[to his attendants]*
                    Seize him.
He's insulting Thebes and me as well.

DIONYSUS
I warn you—you shouldn't tie me up.
I've got my wits about me. You've lost yours.   630

PENTHEUS -
But I'm more powerful than you,
so I'll have you put in chains.

DIONYSUS
                    You're quite ignorant
of why you live, what you do, and who you are.

PENTHEUS
I am Pentheus, son of Agave and Echion.

DIONYSUS
A suitable name. It suggests misfortune.[1]

PENTHEUS *[to his soldiers]*
                       Go now.
Lock him up—in the adjoining stables.
That way he'll see nothing but the darkness.   [510]
There you can dance. As for all those women,
those partners in crime you brought along with you,
we'll sell them off or keep them here as slaves,   640
working our looms, once we've stopped their hands
beating those drum skins, making all that noise.

[Exit Pentheus into the palace, leaving Dionysus with the soldiers]

DIONYSUS
I'll go, then. For I won't have to suffer
what won't occur. But you can be sure of this—
Dionysus, whom you claim does not exist,
will go after you for retribution
after all your insolence. He's the one
you put in chains when you treat me unjustly.

[The soldiers lead Dionysus away to an area beside the palace]

CHORUS
O Sacred Dirce, blessed maiden,
daughter of Achelous,   650   [520]
your streams once received
the new-born child of Zeus,
when his father snatched him
from those immortal fires,
then hid him in his thigh,
crying out these words,
"Go, Dithyrambus,
enter my male womb.
I'll make you known as Bacchus

[1]The name Pentheus is linked to the Greek word for *suffering* or *misfortune*.

29

to all those in Thebes, 660
who'll invoke you with that name."
But you, O sacred Dirce, [530]
why do you resist me,
my garland-bearing company,
along your river banks?
Why push me away?
Why seek to flee from me?
I tell you, you'll find joy
in grape-filled vines from Dionysus.
They'll make you love him. 670

What rage, what rage
shows up in that earth-bound race
of Pentheus, born to Echion, [540]
an earth-bound mortal.
He's descended from a snake,
that Pentheus, a savage beast,
not a normal mortal man,
but some bloody monster
who fights against the gods.
He'll soon bind me in chains, 680
as a worshipper of Bacchus.
Already he holds in his house
my fellow Bacchic revelers,
hidden there in some dark cell.
Do you see, Dionysus,
child of Zeus, your followers [550]
fighting their oppression?
Come down, my lord,
down from Olympus,
wave your golden thyrsus, 690
to cut short the profanities
of this blood-thirsty man.

Where on Mount Nysa,
which nourishes wild beasts,

where on the Corcyrean heights,
where do you wave your thyrsus
over your worshippers,
O Dionysus?
Perhaps in those thick woods   [560]
of Mount Olympus,   700
where Orpheus once played his lyre,
brought trees together with his songs,
collecting wild beasts round him.
O blessed Peiria,
whom Dionysus loves—
he'll come to set you dancing
in the Bacchic celebrations.
He'll cross the foaming Axius,
lead his whirling Maenads on,   [570]
leaving behind the river Lydias   710
which enriches mortal men,
and which, they say, acts as a father,
nourishing with many lovely streams
a land where horses flourish.

*[The soldiers move in to round up the chorus of Bacchae. As they do
so, the ground begins to shake, thunder sounds, lightning flashes,
and the entire palace starts to break apart]*

DIONYSUS *[shouting from within]*
   Io! Hear me, hear me as I call you.
   Io! Bacchae! Io Bacchae!

CHORUS *[a confusion of different voices]*
   Who's that? Who is it? It's Dionysus' voice!
   It's calling me. But from what direction?

DIONYSUS *[from within]*
   Io! Io! I'm calling out again—   [580]
   the son of Semele, a child of Zeus!   720

31

CHORUS
Io! Io! Lord and master!
Come join our company,
Bromius, O Bromius!

DIONYSUS *[from within]*
Sacred lord of earthquakes, shake this ground.

[The earthquake tremors resume]

CHORUS VOICE 1
Ai! Soon Pentheus' palace
will be shaken into rubble.

CHORUS VOICE 2
Dionysus is in the house—revere him.

CHORUS VOICE 3
We revere him, we revere him.   [590]

CHORUS VOICE 4
You see those stone lintels on the pillars—
they're splitting up. It's Bromius calling,   730
shouting to us from inside the walls.

DIONYSUS *[from within]*
Let fiery lightning strike right now—
burn Pentheus' palace—consume it all!

CHORUS VOICE 5
Look! Don't you see the fire—
there by the sacred tomb of Semele!
The flame left by that thunderbolt from Zeus,
when the lightning flash destroyed her,
all that time ago. O Maenads—
throw your bodies on the ground, down, down,   [600]
for our master, Zeus' son, moves now   740
against the palace—to demolish it.

32

[Enter Dionysus, bursting through the palace front doors, free of all chains, smiling and supremely confident.]

DIONYSUS

Ah, my barbarian Asian women,
Do you lie prostate on the ground with fear?
It seems you feel Dionysus' power,
as he rattles Pentheus' palace.
Get up now. Be brave. And stop your trembling.

CHORUS LEADER

How happy I am to see you—
Our greatest light in all the joyful dancing.
We felt alone and totally abandoned.

DIONYSUS

Did you feel despair when I was sent away,   750   [610]
cast down in Pentheus' gloomy dungeon?

CHORUS LEADER

How could I not? Who'll protect me
if you run into trouble? But tell me,
how did you escape that ungodly man?

DIONYSUS

No trouble. I saved myself with ease.

CHORUS LEADER

But didn't he bind up your hands up in chains?

DIONYSUS

In this business I was playing with him—
he thought he was tying me up, the fool!
He didn't even touch or handle me,
he was so busy feeding his desires.   760
In that stable where he went to tie me up,
he found a bull. He threw the iron fetters
around its knees and hooves. As he did so,
he kept panting in his rage, dripping sweat   [620]

33

from his whole body—his teeth gnawed his lip.
I watched him, sitting quietly nearby.
After a while, Bacchus came and shook the place,
setting his mother Semele's tomb on fire.
Seeing that, Pentheus thought his palace
was burning down. He ran round, here and there,   770
yelling to his slaves to bring more water.
His servants set to work—and all for nothing!
Once I'd escaped, he ended all that work.
Seizing a dark sword, he rushed inside the house.
Then, it seems to me, but I'm guessing now,
Bromius set up out there in the courtyard   [630]
some phantom image. Pentheus charged it,
slashing away at nothing but bright air,
thinking he was butchering me. There's more—
Bacchus kept hurting him in still more ways.   780
He knocked his house down, right to the ground,
all shattered. So Pentheus has witnessed
a bitter end to my imprisonment.
He's dropped his sword, worn out, exhausted,
a mere mortal daring to fight a god.
So now I've strolled out calmly to you,
leaving the house, ignoring Pentheus.
Wait! It seems to me I hear marching feet—
no doubt he'll come out front here soon enough.
What will he say, I wonder, after this?   790
Well, I'll deal with him quite gently,   [640]
even if he comes out breathing up a storm.
After all, a wise man ought to keep his temper.

[Pentheus comes hurriedly out of the palace, accompanied by armed soldiers]

PENTHEUS
    What's happening to me—total disaster!
    The stranger's gone, and we'd just chained him up.

34

[Seeing Dionysus]

Ah ha! Here is the man—right here.
What's going on? How did you get out?
How come you're here, outside my palace?

DIONYSUS
Hold on. Calm down. Don't be so angry.

PENTHEUS
How did you escape your chains and get here?   800

DIONYSUS
Didn't I say someone would release me—
or did you miss that part?

PENTHEUS
                    Who was it?   [650]
You're always explaining things in riddles.

DIONYSUS
It was the one who cultivates for men
the richly clustering vine.

PENTHEUS
                    Ah, this Dionysus.
Your words are a lovely insult to your god.

DIONYSUS
He came to Thebes with nothing but good things.

PENTHEUS *[To soldiers]*
Seal off all the towers on my orders—
all of them around the city.

DIONYSUS
                    What for?
Surely a god can make it over any wall?   810

35

PENTHEUS
You're so wise, except in all those things
in which you should be wise.

DIONYSUS
              I was born wise,
especially in matters where I need to be.

[Enter the Messenger, a cattle herder from the hills]

But first you'd better listen to this man,
hear what he has to say, for he's come here
from the mountains to report to you.
I'll still be here for you. I won't run off.

MESSENGER
Pentheus, ruler of this land of Thebes,   [660]
I've just left Cithaeron, that mountain
where the sparkling snow never melts away.   820

PENTHEUS
What this important news you've come with?

MESSENGER
I saw those women in their Bacchic revels,
those sacred screamers, all driven crazy,
the ones who run barefoot from their homes.
I came, my lord, to tell you and the city
the dreadful things they're doing—their actions
are beyond all wonder. But, my lord,
first I wish to know if I should tell you,
openly report what's going on up there,
or whether I should hold my tongue.   830
Your mood changes so fast I get afraid—   [670]
your sharp spirit, your all-too-royal temper.

PENTHEUS
Speak on. Whatever you have to report,
you'll get no punishment at all from me.

36

It's not right to vent one's anger on the just.
The more terrible the things you tell me
about those Bacchic women, the worse
I'll move against the one who taught them
all their devious tricks.

MESSENGER

The grazing cattle
were just moving into upland pastures,   840
at the hour the sun sends out its beams
to warm the earth. Right then I saw them—
three groups of dancing women. One of them   [680]
Autonoe led. Your mother, Agave,
led the second group, and Ino led the third.[1]
They were all asleep, bodies quite relaxed,
some leaning back on leafy boughs of pine,
others cradling heads on oak-leaf pillows,
resting on the ground—in all modesty.
They weren't as you described—all drunk on wine   850
or on the music of their flutes, hunting
for Aphrodite in the woods alone.
Once she heard my horned cattle lowing,
your mother stood up amid those Bacchae,
then called them to stir their limbs from sleep.
They rubbed refreshing sleep out of their eyes,   [690]
and stood up straight there—a marvelous sight,
to see such an orderly arrangement,
women young and old and still unmarried girls.
First, they let their hair loose down their shoulders,   860
tied up the fawn skins (some had undone the knots
to loosen up the chords). Then around those skins
they looped some snakes, who licked the women's cheeks.
Some held young gazelles or wild wolf cubs
and fed them on their own white milk, the ones   [700]
who'd left behind at home a new-born child,

[1]Autonoe and Ino are sisters of Pentheus' mother, Agave, hence Pentheus'
aunts.

whose breasts were still swollen full of milk.
They draped themselves with garlands from oak trees,
ivy, and flowering yew. Then one of them,
taking a thyrsus, struck a rock with it,   870
and water gushed out, fresh as dew. Another,
using her thyrsus, scraped the ground. At once,
the god sent fountains of wine up from the spot.
All those who craved white milk to drink
just scratched the earth with their fingertips—
it came out in streams. From their ivy wands   [710]
thick, sweet honey dripped. O, if you'd been there,
if you'd seen this, you'd come with reverence
to that god whom you criticize so much.
Well, we cattle herders and shepherds met   880
to discuss and argue with each other
about the astonishing things we'd seen.
And then a man who'd been in town a bit
and had a way with words said to us all,
"You men who live in the holy regions
of these mountains, how'd you like to hunt down
Pentheus' mother, Agave—take her   [720]
away from these Bacchic celebrations,
do the king a favour?" To all of us
he seemed to make good sense. So we set up   890
an ambush, hiding in the bushes,
lying down there. At the appointed time,
the women started their Bacchic ritual,
brandishing the thyrsus and calling out
to the god they cry to, Bromius, Zeus' son.
The entire mountain and its wild animals
were, like them, in one Bacchic ecstasy.
As these women moved, they made all things dance.
Agave, by chance, was dancing close to me.
Leaving the ambush where I'd been concealed,   900
I jumped out, hoping to grab hold of her.   [730]
But she screamed out, "O my quick hounds,

men are hunting us. Come, follow me.
Come on, armed with that thyrsus in your hand."
We ran off, and so escaped being torn apart.
But then those Bacchic women, all unarmed,
went at the heifers browsing on the turf,
using their bare hands. You should have seen one
ripping a fat, young, lowing calf apart—
others tearing cows in pieces with their hands.   910
You could've seen ribs and cloven hooves   [740]
tossed everywhere—some hung up in branches
dripping blood and gore. And bulls, proud beasts till then,
with angry horns, collapsed there on the ground,
dragged down by the hands of a thousand girls.
Hides covering their bodies were stripped off
faster than you could wink your royal eye.
Then, like birds carried up by their own speed,
they rushed along the lower level ground,
beside Asopus' streams, that fertile land   920
which yields its crops to Thebes. Like fighting troops,   [750]
they raided Hysiae and Erythrae,
below rocky Cithaeron, smashing
everything, snatching children from their homes.
Whatever they carried on their shoulders,
even bronze or iron, never tumbled off
onto the dark earth, though nothing was tied down.
They carried fire in their hair, but those flames
never singed them. Some of the villagers,
enraged at being plundered by the Bacchae,   930
seized weapons. The sight of what happened next,   [760]
my lord, was dreadful. For their pointed spears
did not draw blood. But when those women
threw the thrysoi in their hands, they wounded them
and drove them back in flight. The women did this
to men, but not without some god's assistance.
Then they went back to where they'd started from,
those fountains which the god had made for them.

39

They washed off the blood. Snakes licked their cheeks,
cleansing their skin of every drop. My lord,   940
you must welcome this god into our city,
whoever he is. He's a mighty god   [770]
in many other ways. The people say,
so I've heard, he gives to mortal human beings
that vine which puts an end to human grief.
Without wine, there's no more Aphrodite—
or any other pleasure left for men.

CHORUS LEADER
I'm afraid to talk freely before the king,
but nonetheless I'll speak—this Dionysus
is not inferior to any god.   950

PENTHEUS
This Dionysian arrogance, like fire,
keeps flaring up close by—a great insult
to all the Greeks. We must not hesitate.

[To one of his armed attendants]

Go to the Electra Gates. Call out the troops,   [780]
the heavy infantry, all fast cavalry.
Tell them to muster, along with all those
who carry shields—all the archers, too,
the men who pull the bowstring back by hand.
We'll march out against these Bacchae.
In this whole business we will lose control,   960
if we have to put up with what we've suffered
from these women.

DIONYSUS
            You've heard what I had to say,
Pentheus, but still you're not convinced.
Though I'm suffering badly at your hands,
I say you shouldn't go to war against a god.
You should stay calm. Bromius will not let you   [790]

40

move his Bacchae from their mountains.

PENTHEUS
Don't preach to me! You've got out of prison—
enjoy that fact. Or shall I punish you some more?

DIONYSUS
I'd sooner make an offering to that god   970
than in some angry fit kick at his whip—
a mortal going to battle with a god.

PENTHEUS
I'll sacrifice all right—with a slaughter
of those women, just as they deserve—
in the forests on Cithaeron.

DIONYSUS
                                    You'll all run.
What a disgrace! To turn your bronze shields round,
fleeing the thyrsoi of those Bacchic women!

PENTHEUS *[turning to one of his armed attendants, as if to go]*
It's useless trying to argue with this stranger—   [800]
whatever he does or suffers, he won't stay quiet.

DIONYSUS *[calling Pentheus back]*
My lord! There's still a chance to end this calmly.   980

PENTHEUS
By doing what? Should I become a slave
to my own slaves?

DIONYSUS
                        I'll bring the women here—
without the use of any weapons.

PENTHEUS
                                    I don't think so.
You're setting me up for your tricks again.

41

DIONYSUS
What sort of trick, if I want to save you
in my own way?

PENTHEUS
You've made some arrangement,
you and your god, so you can always dance
your Bacchanalian orgies.

DIONYSUS
Yes, that's true.
I have made some arrangement with the god.

PENTHEUS *[to one of his armed servants]*
You there, bring me my weapons.

[to Dionysus]

And you,   990
No more talk! Keep quiet!

DIONYSUS
Just a minute!   [810]
How'd you like to see those women out there,
sitting together in the mountains?

PENTHEUS
I'd like that.
Yes, for that I'd pay in gold—and pay a lot.

DIONYSUS
Why is that? Why do you desire it so much?

PENTHEUS
I'd be sorry to see the women drunk.

DIONYSUS
Would you derive pleasure from looking on,
viewing something you find painful?

PENTHEUS

Yes, I would—
if I were sitting in the trees in silence.

DIONYSUS

But even if you go there secretly,   1000
they'll track you down.

PENTHEUS

You're right.
I'll go there openly.

DIONYSUS

So you're prepared,
are you, to make the trip? Shall I lead you there?

PENTHEUS

Let's go, and with all speed. I've got time.   [820]

DIONYSUS

In that case, you must clothe your body
in a dress—one made of eastern linen.

PENTHEUS

What! I'm not going up there as a man?
I've got to change myself into a woman?

DIONYSUS

If they see you as a man, they'll kill you.

PENTHEUS

Right again. You always have the answer.   1010

DIONYSUS

Dionysus taught me all these things.

PENTHEUS

How can I best follow your suggestion?

43

DIONYSUS
I'll go inside your house and dress you up.

PENTHEUS
What? Dress myself in women's clothing?
I can't do that—I'd be ashamed to.

DIONYSUS
You're still keen to see the Maenads, aren't you?

PENTHEUS
What sort of clothing do you recommend?
How should I cover up my body?   [830]

DIONYSUS
I'll fix up a long hair piece for your head.

PENTHEUS
All right. What's the next piece of my outfit?   1020

DIONYSUS
A dress down to your feet—then a headband,
to fit just here, around your forehead.

PENTHEUS
What else? What other things will you provide?

DIONYSUS
A thyrsus to hold and a dappled fawn skin.

PENTHEUS
No. I can't dress up in women's clothes!

DIONYSUS
But if you go fighting with these Bacchae,
you'll cause bloodshed.

PENTHEUS
                            Yes, that's true.
So first, we must go up and spy on them.

44

DIONYSUS
That's a wiser way to go about this
than hunting evil by committing evil.   1030

PENTHEUS
But how will I make it through the city
without the Thebans noticing me?   [840]

DIONYSUS
We'll go by deserted streets. I'll take you.

PENTHEUS
Well, anything's easier to accept
than being made a fool by Bacchic women.
Let's go in the house. I'll think about what's best.

DIONYSUS
As you wish. Whatever you do, I'm ready.

PENTHEUS
I think I'll go in now. It's a choice
of going with weapons or taking your advice.

[Exit Pentheus into the palace. Dionysus turns to face the chorus]

DIONYSUS
My women! that man's now entangled in our net.   1040
He'll go to those Bacchae, and there he'll die.
That will be his punishment. Dionysus,
you're not far away. Now it's up to you.
Punish him. First, make sure he goes insane   [850]
with some crazed fantasy. If his mind is strong,
he'll not agree to put on women's clothes.
But he'll do it, if you make him mad.
I want him made the laughing stock of Thebes,
while I lead him through the city, mincing
as he moves along dressed as a female,   1050
after he made himself so terrifying
with all those earlier threats. Now I'll be off,

45

to fit Pentheus into the costume
he'll wear when he goes down to Hades,
once he's butchered by his mother's hands.
He'll come to acknowledge Dionysus,
son of Zeus, born in full divinity,   [860]
most fearful, yet most kind to human beings.

[Exit Dionysus]

CHORUS
Oh, when will I be dancing,
leaping barefoot through the night,   1060
flinging back my head in ecstasy,
in the clear, cold, dew-fresh air—
like a playful fawn
celebrating its green joy
across the meadows—
joy that it's escaped the fearful hunt—
as she runs beyond the hunters,
leaping past their woven nets—   [870]
they call out to their hounds
to chase her with still more speed,   1070
but she strains every limb,
racing like a wind storm,
rejoicing by the river plain,
in places where no hunters lurk,
in the green living world
beneath the shady branches,
the foliage of the trees.

What is wisdom? What is finer
than the rights men get from gods—
to hold their powerful hands   1080
over the heads of their enemies?   [880]
Ah yes, what's good is always loved.

The power of the gods
is difficult to stir—

46

but it's a power we can count on.
It punishes all mortal men
who honour their own ruthless wills,
who, in their fits of madness,
fail to reverence the gods.
Gods track down every man   1090
who scorns their worship,
using their cunning to conceal
the enduring steady pace of time.   [890]
For there's no righteousness
in those who recognize or practice
what's beyond our customary laws.
The truth is easy to acknowledge:
whatever is divine is mighty,
whatever has been long-established law
is an eternal natural truth.   1100

What is wisdom? What is finer
than the rights men get from gods—
to hold their powerful hands
over the heads of their enemies?   [900]
Ah yes, what's good is always loved.

Whoever has escaped a storm at sea
is a happy man in harbour,
whoever overcomes great hardship
is likewise another happy man.
Various men outdo each other   1110
in wealth, in power,
in all sorts of ways.
The hopes of countless men
are infinite in number.
Some make men rich;
some come to nothing.
So I consider that man blessed
who lives a happy life   [910]
existing day by day.

47

[Enter Dionysus from the palace. He calls back through the open doors]

DIONYSUS
You who are so desperately eager   1120
to see those things you should not look upon,
so keen to chase what you should not pursue—
I mean you, Pentheus, come out here now,
outside the palace, where I can see you
dressed up as a raving Bacchic female,
to spy upon your mother's company.

[Enter Pentheus dressed in women's clothing. He moves in a deliberately over-stated female way, enjoying the role]

DIONYSUS
You look just like one of Cadmus' daughters.

PENTHEUS
Fancy that! I seem to see two suns,
two images of seven-gated Thebes.
And you look like a bull leading me out here,   1130   [920]
with those horns growing from your head.
Were you once upon a time a beast?
It's certain now you've changed into a bull.

DIONYSUS
The god walks here. He's made a pact with us.
Before his attitude was not so kind.
Now you're seeing just what you ought to see.

PENTHEUS
How do I look? Am I holding myself
just like Ino or my mother, Agave?

DIONYSUS
When I look at you, I think I see them.
But here, this strand of hair is out of place.   1140
It's not under the headband where I fixed it.

48

PENTHEUS *[demonstrating his dancing steps]*
I must have worked it loose inside the house,   [930]
shaking my head when I moved here and there,
practising my Bacchanalian dancing.

DIONYSUS
I'll rearrange it for you. It's only right
that I should serve you. Straighten up your head.

[Dionysus begins adjusting Pentheus' hair and clothing]

PENTHEUS
All right then. You can be my dresser,
now that I've transformed myself for you.

DIONYSUS
Your girdle's loose. And these pleats in your dress
are crooked, too, down at your ankle here.   1150

PENTHEUS *[examining the backs of his legs]*
Yes, that seems to be true for my right leg,
but on this side the dress hangs perfectly,
down the full length of my limb.

DIONYSUS
                Once you see
those Bacchic women acting modestly,
once you confront something you don't expect,   [940]
you'll consider me your dearest friend.

PENTHEUS
This thyrsus—should I hold it in my right hand
or in my left? Which is more suitable
in Bacchic celebrations?

DIONYSUS
                In your right.
You must lift your right foot in time with it.   1160

49

[Dionysus observes Pentheus trying out the dance step]

DIONYSUS
Your mind has changed. I applaud you for it.

PENTHEUS
Will I be powerful enough to carry
the forests of Cithaeron on my shoulders,
along with all those Bacchic females?

DIONYSUS
If you have desire, you'll have the power.
Before this your mind was not well adjusted,
but now it's working in you as it should.

PENTHEUS
Are we going to take some levers with us?
Or shall I rip the forests up by hand,
putting arm and shoulder under mountain peaks?   1170 [950]

DIONYSUS
As long as you don't do away with
those places where the nymphs all congregate,
where Pan plays his music on his pipes.

PENTHEUS
You mention a good point. I'll use no force
to get the better of these women.
I'll conceal myself there in the pine trees.

DIONYSUS
You'll find just the sort of hiding place
a spy should find who wants to hide himself,
so he can gaze upon the Maenads.

PENTHEUS
That's good. I can picture them right now,   1180
in the woods, going at it like rutting birds,
clutching each other as they make sweet love.

50

DIONYSUS

Perhaps. That's why you're going—as a guard
to stop all that. Maybe you'll capture them,   [960]
unless you're captured first.

PENTHEUS

                                    Lead on—
through the centre of our land of Thebes.
I'm the only man in all the city
who dares to undertake this enterprise.

DIONYSUS

You bear the city's burden by yourself,
all by yourself. So your work is waiting there,   1190
the tasks that have been specially set for you.
Follow me. I'm the guide who'll rescue you.
When you return, someone else will bring you back.

PENTHEUS

That will be my mother.

DIONYSUS

                                    For everyone
you'll have become a man to celebrate.

PENTHEUS

That's why I'm going.

DIONYSUS

                            You'll be carried back . . .

PENTHEUS [interrupting]
You're pampering me!

DIONYSUS [continuing]
                            . . . in your mother's arms.

PENTHEUS
You've really made up your mind to spoil me.

51

DIONYSUS
To spoil you? That's true, but in my own way.

PENTHEUS
Then I'll be off to get what I deserve.   1200   [970]

[Exit Pentheus]

DIONYSUS
You fearful, terrifying man—on your way
to horrific suffering. Well, you'll win
a towering fame, as high as heaven.
Hold out your hand to him, Agave,
you, too, her sisters, Cadmus' daughters.
I'm leading this young man in your direction,
for the great confrontation, where I'll triumph—
I and Bromius. What else will happen
events will show, as they occur.

[Exit Dionysus]

CHORUS
Up now, you hounds of madness,   1210
go up now into the mountains,
go where Cadmus' daughters
keep their company of worshippers,   [980]
goad them into furious revenge
against that man, that raving spy,
all dressed up in his women's clothes,
so keen to glimpse the Maenads.
His mother will see him first,
as he spies on them in secret
from some level rock or crag.   1220
She'll scream out to her Maenads,
"Who's the man who's come here,
to the mountains, to these mountains,
tracking Cadmean mountain dancers?
O my Bacchae, who has come?

52

From whom was this man born?
He's not born of woman's blood—
he must be some lioness' whelp
or spawned from Libyan gorgons."   [990]

Let justice manifest itself—   1230
let justice march, sword in hand,
to stab him in the throat,
that godless, lawless man,
unjust earthborn seed of Echion.

Any man intent on wickedness,
turning his unlawful rage
against your rites, O Bacchus,
against the worship of your mother,
a man who sets out with an insane mind,   [1000]
his courage founded on a falsehood,   1240
who seeks to overcome by force
what simply can't be overcome—
let death set his intentions straight.
For a life devoid of grief is one
which receives without complaint
whatever comes down from the gods—
that's how mortals ought to live.
Wisdom is something I don't envy.
My joy comes hunting other things
lofty and plain to everyone.   1250
They lead man's life to good
in purity and reverence,
honouring gods day and night,
eradicating from our lives
customs lying beyond what's right.   [1010]

Let justice manifest itself—
let justice march, sword in hand,
to stab him in the throat,
that godless, lawless man,

53

unjust earthborn seed of Echion.   1260

Appear now to our sight, O Bacchus—
come as a bull or many-headed serpent
or else some fire-breathing lion.
Go now, Bacchus, with your smiling face   [1020]
cast your deadly noose upon
that hunter of the Bacchae,
as the group of Maenads brings him down.

[Enter Second Messenger, one of Pentheus' attendants]

SECOND MESSENGER
How I grieve for this house, in earlier days
so happy throughout Greece, home of that old man,
Cadmus from Sidon, who sowed the fields   1270
to harvest the earth-born crop produced
from serpent Ophis. How I now lament—
I know I'm just a slave, but nonetheless . . .

CHORUS
Do you bring us news?
Has something happened,
something about the Bacchae?

SECOND MESSENGER
Pentheus, child of Echion, is dead.   [1030]

CHORUS
O my lord Bromius,
Now your divine greatness
is here made manifest!   1280

SECOND MESSENGER
What are you saying? Why that song?
Women, how can you now rejoice like this
for the death of one who was my master?

54

CHORUS LEADER
We're strangers here in Thebes,
so we sing out our joy
in chants from foreign lands.
No longer need we cower here
in fear of prisoner's chains.

SECOND MESSENGER
Do you think Thebes lacks sufficient men
to take care of your punishment?   1290

CHORUS
Dionysus, O Dionysus,
he's the one with power over me—
not Thebes.

SECOND MESSENGER
That you may be forgiven, but to cry
aloud with joy when such disasters come,
women, that's not something you should do.   [1040]

CHORUS
Speak to me, tell all—
How did death strike him down,
that unrighteous man,
that man who acted so unjustly?   1300

SECOND MESSENGER
Once we'd left the settlements of Thebes,
we went across the river Asopus,
then started the climb up Mount Cithaeron—
Pentheus and myself, I following the king.
The stranger was our guide, scouting the way.
First, we sat down in a grassy meadow,
keeping our feet and tongues quite silent,
so we could see without being noticed.   [1050]
There was a valley there shut in by cliffs.
Through it refreshing waters flowed, with pines   1310

55

providing shade. The Maenads sat there,
their hands all busy with delightful work—
some of them with ivy strands repairing
damaged thyrsoi, while others sang,
chanting Bacchic songs to one another,
carefree as fillies freed from harness.
Then Pentheus, that unhappy man,
not seeing the crowd of women, spoke up,
"Stranger, I can't see from where we're standing.
My eyes can't glimpse those crafty Maenads.   1320 [1060]
But up there, on that hill, a pine tree stands.
If I climbed that, I might see those women,
and witness the disgraceful things they do."
Then I saw that stranger work a marvel.
He seized that pine tree's topmost branch—
it stretched up to heaven—and brought it down,
pulling it to the dark earth, bending it
as if it were a bow or some curved wheel
forced into a circle while staked out with pegs—
that's how the stranger made that tree bend down,   1330
forcing the mountain pine to earth by hand,
something no mortal man could ever do.
He set Pentheus in that pine tree's branches.   [1070]
Then his hands released the tree, but slowly,
so it stood up straight, being very careful
not to shake Pentheus loose. So that pine
towered straight up to heaven, with my king
perched on its back. Maenads could see him there
more easily than he could spy on them.
As he was just becoming visible—   1340
the stranger had completely disappeared—
some voice—I guess it was Dionysus—
cried out from the sky, "Young women,
I've brought you the man who laughed at you,   [1080]
who ridiculed my rites. Now punish him!"
As he shouted this, a dreadful fire arose,

56

blazing between the earth and heaven.
The air was still. In the wooded valley
no sound came from the leaves, and all the beasts
were silent, too. The women stood up at once.   1350
They'd heard the voice, but not distinctly.
They gazed around them. Then again the voice
shouted his commands. When Cadmus' daughters
clearly heard what Dionysus ordered,
they rushed out, running as fast as doves,   [1090]
moving their feet at an amazing speed.
His mother Agave with both her sisters
and all the Bacchae charged straight through
the valley, the torrents, the mountain cliffs,
pushed to a god-inspired frenzy.   1360
They saw the king there sitting in that pine.
First, they scaled a cliff face looming up
opposite the tree and started throwing rocks,
trying to hurt him. Others threw branches,
or hurled their thyrsoi through the air at him,
sad, miserable Pentheus, their target.   [1100]
But they didn't hit him. The poor man
sat high beyond their frantic cruelty,
trapped up there, no way to save his skin.
Then, like lightning, they struck oak branches down,   1370
trying them as levers to uproot the tree.
When these attempts all failed, Agave said,
"Come now, make a circle round the tree.
Then, Maenads, each of you must seize a branch,
so we can catch the climbing beast up there,
stop him making our god's secret dances known."
Thousands of hands grabbed the tree and pulled.
They yanked it from the ground. Pentheus fell,   [1110]
crashing to earth down from his lofty perch,
screaming in distress. He knew well enough   1380
something dreadful was about to happen.
His priestess mother first began the slaughter.

57

She hurled herself at him. Pentheus tore off
his headband, untying it from his head,
so wretched Agave would recognize him,
so she wouldn't kill him. Touching her cheek,
he cried out, "It's me, mother, Pentheus,
your child. You gave birth to me at home,
in Echion's house. Pity me, mother—   [1120]
don't kill your child because I've made mistakes."   1390
But Agave was foaming at the mouth,
eyes rolling in their sockets, her mind not set
on what she ought to think—she didn't listen—
she was possessed, in a Bacchic frenzy.
She seized his left arm, below the elbow,
pushed her foot against the poor man's ribs,
then tore his shoulder out. The strength she had—
it was not her own. The god put power
into those hands of hers. Meanwhile Ino,
her sister, went at the other side,   1400
ripping off chunks of Pentheus' flesh,
while Autonoe and all the Bacchae,   [1130]
the whole crowd of them, attacked as well,
all of them howling out together.
As long as Pentheus was still alive,
he kept on screaming. The women cried in triumph—
one brandished an arm, another held a foot—
complete with hunting boot—the women's nails
tore his ribs apart. Their hands grew bloody,
tossing bits of flesh back and forth, for fun.   1410
His body parts lie scattered everywhere—
some under rough rocks, some in the forest,
deep in the trees. They're difficult to find.
As for the poor victim's head, his mother   [1140]
stumbled on it. Her hands picked it up,
then stuck it on a thyrsus, at the tip.
Now she carries it around Cithaeron,
as though it were some wild lion's head.

58

She's left her sisters dancing with the Maenads.
She's coming here, inside these very walls,   1420
showing off with pride her ill-fated prey,
calling out to her fellow hunter, Bacchus,
her companion in the chase, the winner,
the glorious victor. By serving him,
in her great triumph she wins only tears.
As for me, I'm leaving this disaster,
before Agave gets back home again.
The best thing is to keep one's mind controlled,   [1150]
and worship all that comes down from the gods.
That, in my view, is the wisest custom,   1430
for those who can conduct their lives that way.

[Exit Messenger]

CHORUS
Let's dance to honour Bacchus,
Let's shout to celebrate what's happened here,
happened to Pentheus,
child of the serpent,
who put on women's clothes,
who took up the beautiful and blessed thyrsus—
his certain death,
disaster brought on by the bull.
You Bacchic women   1440   [1160]
descended from old Cadmus,
you've won glorious victory,
one which ends in tears,
which ends in lamentation.
A noble undertaking this,
to drench one's hands in blood,
life blood dripping from one's only son.

CHORUS LEADER
Wait! I see Agave, Pentheus' mother,
on her way home, her eyes transfixed.

59

Let's now welcome her,   1450
the happy revels of our god of joy!

[Enter Agave, cradling the head of Pentheus]

AGAVE
   Asian Bacchae . . .

CHORUS
                     Why do you appeal to me?

AGAVE *[displaying the head]*
   From the mountains I've brought home   [1170]
   this ivy tendril freshly cut.
   We've had a blessed hunt.

CHORUS
                        I see it.
   As your fellow dancer, I'll accept it.

AGAVE
   I caught this young lion without a trap,
   as you can see.

CHORUS
                  What desert was he in?

AGAVE
   Cithaeron.

CHORUS
               On Cithaeron?

AGAVE
   Cithaeron killed him.

CHORUS
                    Who struck him down?   1460

AGAVE

The honour of the first blow goes to me.
In the dancing I'm called blessed Agave. [1180

CHORUS

Who else?

AGAVE

Well, from Cadmus . . .

CHORUS

From Cadmus what?

AGAVE

His other children laid hands on the beast,
but after me—only after I did first.
We've had good hunting. So come, share our feast.

CHORUS

What? You want me to eat that with you?
O you unhappy woman!

AGAVE

This is a young bull. Look at this cheek
It's just growing downy under the crop 1470
of his soft hair.

CHORUS

His hair makes him resemble
some wild beast.

AGAVE

Bacchus is a clever huntsman— [1190]
he wisely set his Maenads on this beast.

CHORUS

Yes, our master is indeed a hunter.

AGAVE

Have you any praise for me?

61

CHORUS
                    I praise you.

AGAVE
Soon all Cadmus' people . . .

CHORUS
                    . . . and Pentheus, your son, as well.

AGAVE
. . . will celebrate his mother, who caught the beast,
just like a lion.

CHORUS
                    It's a strange trophy.

AGAVE
And strangely captured, too.

CHORUS
                    You're proud of what you've done?

AGAVE
Yes, I'm delighted. Great things I've done—   1480
great things on this hunt, clear for all to see.

CHORUS
Well then, you most unfortunate woman,   [1200]
show off your hunting prize, your sign of victory,
to all the citizens.

AGAVE *[addressing everyone]*
                    All of you here,
all you living in the land of Thebes,
in this city with its splendid walls,
come see this wild beast we hunted down—
daughters of Cadmus—not with thonged spears,
Thessalian javelins, or by using nets,
but with our own white hands, our finger tips.   1490

After this, why should huntsmen boast aloud,
when no one needs the implements they use?
We caught this beast by hand, tore it apart— [1210]
with our own hands. But where's my father?
He should come here. And where's Pentheus?
Where is my son? He should take a ladder,
set it against the house, fix this lion's head
way up there, high on the palace front.
I've captured it and brought it home with me.

[Enter Cadmus and attendants, carrying parts of Pentheus' body]

CADMUS
Follow me, all those of you who carry   1500
some part of wretched Pentheus. You slaves,
come here, right by the house.

[They place the bits of Pentheus' body together in a chest front of the palace]

                              I'm worn out.
So many searches—but I picked up the body.
I came across it in the rocky clefts
on Mount Cithaeron, ripped to pieces,   [1220]
no parts lying together in one place.
It was in the woods—difficult to search.
Someone told me what my daughter's done,
those horrific acts, once I came back,
returning here with old Tiresias,   1510
inside the city walls, back from the Bacchae.
So I climbed the mountains once again.
Now I bring home this child the Maenads killed.
I saw Autonoe, who once bore
Actaeon to Aristaeus—and Ino,
she was with her there, in the forest,
both still possessed, quite mad, poor creatures.
Someone said Agave was coming here,   [1230]
still doing her Bacchic dance. He spoke the truth,

for I see her there—what a wretched sight!

AGAVE
Father, now you can be truly proud.
Among all living men you've produced
by far the finest daughters. I'm talking
of all of us, but especially of myself.
I've left behind my shuttle and my loom,
and risen to great things, catching wild beasts
with my bare hands. Now I've captured him,
I'm holding in my arms the finest trophy,
as you can see, bringing it back home to you,
so it may hang here.

[offering him Pentheus' head]

                          Take this, father   1530 [1240]
let your hands welcome it. Be proud of it,
of what I've caught. Summon all your friends—
have a banquet, for you are blessed indeed,
blessed your daughters have achieved these things.

CADMUS
This grief's beyond measure, beyond endurance.
With these hands of yours you've murdered him.
You strike down this sacrificial victim,
this offering to the gods, then invite me,
and all of Thebes, to share a banquet.
Alas—first for your sorrow, then my own.   1540
Lord god Bromius, born into this family,
has destroyed us, acting out his justice,   [1250]
but too much so.

AGAVE
                       Why such scowling eyes?
How sorrowful and solemn old men become.
As for my son, I hope he's a fine huntsman,
who copies his mother's hunting style,

when he rides out with young men of Thebes
chasing after creatures in the wild.
The only thing he seems capable of doing
is fighting with the gods. It's up to you,   1550
father, to reprimand him for it.
Who'll call him here into my sight,
so he can see my good luck for himself?

CADMUS
Alas! Alas! What dreadful pain you'll feel
when you recognize what you've just done.   [1260]
If you stay forever in your present state,
you'll be unfortunate, but you won't feel
as if you're suffering unhappiness.

AGAVE
But what in all this is wrong or painful?

CADMUS
First, raise your eyes. Look up into the sky.   1560

AGAVE
All right. But why tell me to look up there?

CADMUS
Does the sky still seem the same to you,
or has it changed?

ΑGAVE
                    It seems, well . . . brighter . . .
more illuminated than it was before.

CADMUS
And your inner spirit—is it still shaking?

AGAVE
I don't understand what it is you're asking.
But my mind is starting to clear somehow.
It's changing . . . it's not what it was before.   [1270]

65

CADMUS
Can you hear me? Can you answer clearly?

AGAVE
Yes. But, father, what we discussed before,   1570
I've quite forgotten.

CADMUS
                                        Then tell me this—
to whose house did you come when you got married?

AGAVE
You gave me to Echion, who, men say,
was one of those who grew from seeds you cast.

CADMUS
In that house you bore your husband a child.
What was his name?

AGAVE
                        His name was Pentheus.
I conceived him with his father.

CADMUS
                                        Well then,
this head your hands are holding—whose is it?

AGAVE
It's a lion's. That's what the hunters said.

CADMUS
Inspect it carefully. You can do that   1580
without much effort.

AGAVE [inspecting the head]
                        What is this?
What am I looking at? What am I holding?   [1280]

CADMUS
Look at it. You'll understand more clearly.

66

AGAVE
What I see fills me with horrific pain . . .
such agony . . .

CADMUS
Does it still seem to you
to be a lion's head?

AGAVE
No. It's appalling—
this head I'm holding belongs to Pentheus.

CADMUS
Yes, that's right. I was lamenting his fate
before you recognized him.

AGAVE
Who killed him?
How did he come into my hands?

CADMUS
Harsh truth—   1590
how you come to light at the wrong moment!

AGAVE
Tell me. My heart is pounding in me
to hear what you're about to say.

CADMUS
You killed him—
you and your sisters.

AGAVE
Where was he killed?
At home? In what sort of place?   [1290]

CADMUS
He was killed
where dogs once made a common meal of Actaeon.

AGAVE

Why did this poor man go to Cithaeron?

CADMUS

He went there to ridicule the god
and you for celebrating Dionysus.

AGAVE

But how did we happen to be up there?

CADMUS

You were insane—the entire city   1600
was in a Bacchic madness.

AGAVE

                    Now I see.
Dionysus has destroyed us all.

CADMUS

He took offense at being insulted.
You did not consider him a god.

AGAVE

Father, where's the body of my dearest son?

CADMUS

I had trouble tracking down the body.
I brought back what I found.

AGAVE

                    Are all his limbs laid out
just as they should be? And Pentheus,   [1300]
what part did he play in my madness?

CADMUS

Like you, he was irreverent to the god.   1610
That's why the god linked you and him together
in the same disaster—thus destroying
the house and me, for I've no children left,

68

now I see this offspring of your womb,
you unhappy woman, cruelly butchered
in the most shameful way. He was the one
who brought new vision to our family.

[Addressing the remains of Pentheus]

My child, you upheld the honour of our house,
my daughter's son. You were feared in Thebes.   [1310]
No one who saw you ever would insult me,   1620
though I was old, for you would then inflict
fit punishment. Now the mighty Cadmus,
the man who sowed and later harvested
the most splendid crop—the Theban people—
will be an exile, banished from his home,
a dishonoured man. Dearest of men,
even though, my child, you're alive no more,
I count you among those closest to me.
You won't be touching my cheek any more,
holding me in your arms, and calling me   1630
"grandfather," as you ask me, "Old man,
who's injuring or dishonouring you?   [1320]
Who upsets your heart with any pain?
Tell me, father, so I can punish him—
anyone who treats you in an unjust way."
Now you're in this horrifying state,
I'm in misery, your mother's pitiful,
and all your relatives are in despair.
If there's a man who disrespects the gods,
let him think about how this man perished—   1640
then he should develop faith in them.

CHORUS LEADER
I'm sorry for you Cadmus—you're in pain.
But your grandson deserved his punishment.

69

AGAVE

Father, you see how all has changed for me.[1]
[From being your royal and honoured daughter,
the mother of a king, I'm now transformed—
an abomination, something to fill
all people's hearts with horror, with disgust—
the mother who slaughtered her only son,
who tore him apart, ripping out the heart   1650
from the child who filled her own heart with joy—
all to honour this god Dionysus.
But, father, give me your permission now
to lay out here the body of my son,
prepare his corpse for proper burial.

CADMUS

That is no easy task to undertake.
His body, all the parts I could collect,
lies here, in this chest, not a pretty sight.
My own eyes can hardly bear to see him.
But if you think you can endure the work,   1660
then, my child, begin the appropriate rites.

[Agave starts taking Pentheus' limbs out of the chest and placing them on the ground in front of her]

AGAVE

Alas, for my poor son, my only child,
destroyed by his mother's Bacchic madness.
How could these hands of mine, which loved him so,
have torn these limbs apart, ripped out his flesh?
Here's an arm which has held me all these years,
growing stronger as he grew into a man,
his feet . . . O how he used to run to me,
seeking assurance of his mother's love.
His face was handsome, on the verge of manhood.   1670

---

[1] At this point there is an important gap in the manuscript. The reconstructed text, which ends at line 1699, appears between square brackets.

See the soft down still resting on these lips,
which have kissed me thousands of times or more.
All this, and all the rest, set here before us.
O Zeus and all you Olympian gods . . . .

[She cannot complete the ritual and collapses in grief]

It makes no sense—it's unendurable.
How could the god have wished such things on me?

CHORUS LEADER
Lady, you must bear what cannot be borne.
Your suffering is intense, but the god is just.
You insulted him in Thebes, showed no respect—
you've brought the punishment upon yourself.   1680

CHORUS
What is wisdom? What is finer
than the rights men get from gods—
to hold their powerful hands
over the heads of their enemies?
Ah yes, what's good is always loved.
So all praise Dionysus,
praise the dancing god,
god of our revelry,
god whose justice is divine,
whose justice now reveals itself.   1690

[Enter Dionysus]

DIONYSUS
Yes, I am Dionysus, son of Zeus.
You see me now before you as a god.
You Thebans learned about my powers too late.
Dishonouring me, you earn the penalty.
You refused my rites. Now you must leave—
abandon your city for barbarian lands.
Agave, too, that polluted creature,

71

must go into perpetual banishment.
And Cadmus, you too must endure your lot.]¹
Your form will change, so you become a dragon.   1700 [1330]
Your wife, Harmonia, Ares' daughter,
whom you, though mortal, took in marriage,
will be transformed, changing to a snake.
As Zeus' oracle declares, you and she
will drive a chariot drawn by heifers.
You'll rule barbarians. With your armies,
too large to count, you'll raze many cities.
Once they despoil Apollo's oracle,
they'll have a painful journey back again.
But Ares will guard you and Harmonia.   1710
In lands of the blessed he'll transform your lives.
That's what I proclaim—I, Dionysus,   [1340]
born from no mortal father, but from Zeus.
If you had understood how to behave
as you should have when you were unwilling,
you'd now be fortunate, with Zeus' child
among your allies.

CADMUS
                              O Dionysus,
we implore you—we've not acted justly.

DIONYSUS
You learn too late. You were ignorant
when you should have known.

CADMUS
                              Now we understand.   1720
Your actions against us are too severe.

DIONYSUS
I was born a god, and you insulted me.

CADMUS

¹The reconstructed text inserted to repair the gap in the manuscript ends here.

72

Angry gods should not act just like humans.

DIONYSUS
My father Zeus willed all this long ago.

AGAVE
Alas, old man, then this must be our fate,   [1350]
a miserable exile.

DIONYSUS
                        Why then delay?
Why postpone what necessity requires?

CADMUS
Child, we've stumbled into this disaster,
this terrible calamity—you and me,
both in agony—your sisters, too.   1730
So I'll go out to the barbarians,
a foreign resident in my old age.
And then for me there is that oracle
which says I'll lead a mixed barbarian force
back into Greece. And I'll bring here with me
Harmonia, Ares' daughter, my wife.
I'll have the savage nature of a snake,
as I lead my soldiers to the altars,
to the tombs, in Greece. But even then,
there'll be no end to my wretched sorrows.   1740 [1360]
I'll never sail the downward plunging Acheron
and reach some final peace.[1]

AGAVE [embracing Cadmus]
Father, I must be exiled without you.

CADMUS
Why do you throw your arms about me,
my unhappy child, just like some young swan
protecting an old one— gray and helpless?

[1]The Acheron is one of the principal rivers of the Underworld.

73

AGAVE
Because I've no idea where to go,
once I'm banished from my father's land.

CADMUS
Child, I don't know. Your father's not much help.

AGAVE
Farewell, then, to my home.   1750
Farewell to my native city.
In my misfortune I abandon you,
an exile from spaces once my own.   [1370]

CADMUS
Go now to Aristaeus' house, my child.[1]

AGAVE
How I grieve for you, my father.

CADMUS
And I grieve for you, my child,
as I weep for your sisters.

AGAVE
Lord Dionysus has inflicted
such brutal terror on your house.

DIONYSUS
Yes. For at your hands I suffered, too—   1760
and dreadfully. For here in Thebes
my name received no recognition.

AGAVE
Farewell, father.

CADMUS
              My most unhappy daughter,
may you fare well. That will be hard for you.   [1380]

[1]Aristeus is the husband of Autonoe and thus Agave's brother-in-law.

74

AGAVE
Lead on, friends, so I may take my sisters,
those pitiful women, into exile with me.
May I go somewhere where cursed Cithaeron
will never see me, nor my eyes glimpse
that dreadful mountain, a place far away
from any sacred thyrsus. Let others   1770
make Bacchic celebrations their concern.

[Exit Agave]

CHORUS
The gods appear in many forms,
carrying with them unwelcome things.
What people thought would happen never did.
What they did not expect, the gods made happen.
That's what this story has revealed.

[Exeunt Chorus and Cadmus, leaving on stage the remains of
Pentheus' body]

Other Translations by Ian Johnston available from Richer Resources Publications

Aeschylus, *Oresteia*

Aristophanes, *Birds*

Aristophanes, *Clouds*

Aristophanes, *Frogs*

Aristophanes, *Lysistrata*

Aristophanes, *Peace*

Euripides, *Medea*

Homer, *Iliad* (complete and abridged editions)

Homer, *Odyssey* (complete and abridged editions)

Kant, *Universal History and Nature of the Heavens*

Nietzsche, *Beyond Good and Evil*

Nietzsche, *Genealogy of Morals*

Sophocles, *Antigone*

Sophocles, *Oedipus the King*

Sophocles, *Philoctetes.*

To inquire about these titles, please use the web address given on the copyright page of this book.

The translations of Homer are available as sound recordings (complete and abridged) from Naxos Audiobooks, as is a complete translation of Friedrich Nietzsche, *Beyond Good and Evil.*

All of these titles are available for pre-viewing and purchase at:

www.RicherResourcesPublications.com